POESY PATE

POESY PATE

Natasha North

CONTENTS

PROLOGUE 1

SEED 3

Pea 5
Maiden 6
Small 9
Wood 10
Dormant 12
Spring 13
Hidden 14
Stir 15
Pare 16
New 18
Morning 19
Bee 20

GROW 25

Crescent 27
Pocket 28
Fire 30
Due 31
River 32
Noon 34
Summer 36
Clay 37
Steady 38
Lover 42
Go 43
Sail 44

FLOWER 47

Autumn 49
Impe 50
Womb 52
Mother 54
Promise 55
Reach 56
Metal 58
Evening 61
Furrow 62
Gibbous 64
Bloom 66
Chance 69

FRUIT 71

Peel 73
Full 74
Reap 77
Winter 78
Crone 80
Carry 81
Night 82
Husk 84
Time 86
Lost 88
Expanse 90
Water 92

EPILOGUE 97

PROLOGUE

A poesy pate:
Each flower's fate,
with petals plucked,
to feed your prose.

She loves me,
or she loves me not.
Before – besotted.
Now – only rotted.

And roses red,
plucked bald and dead.
Poems, petals, heads –
all decompose.

SEED

Pea

Did the princess ever have second thoughts?
Did the castle feel constricting?
Did she notice Charming's chin stubble?
Or did she really live happily ever,
after getting what she wanted?
Or did what she wanted change?
And did she get wise in time
to do something
different?

Or did she shove her second thoughts
and unrequited dreams
down deep under
a hundred feather mattresses
until they felt so small –
an insignificant pebble of a pea –
only mildly irritating
and only if she focused on it
during sleepless nights?

Maiden

When I am small,
I notice my mother's hands.

Her hands hold paper so delicately, like a feather,
as she cuts sure, straight lines
with scissors as extensions of graceful fingers.

Her hands spread peanut butter on white bread,
fold in half, eat one bird bite from the corner,
then leave it out while she tidies some mess, distracted.

Her hands point to each letter of a word,
energy pouring from fingertips like magic spells
to make me see books come alive.

Her hands have rings which I twirl to see gems sparkle.
Her hands sneak dainty trails through my fine, long hair
and leave an echo as my scalp tingles warmly.

Sometimes hands are flowers – so open,
a whisper with no weight to them.
In every touch, conceding.

How fragile fingers
can let things slip
through weakened grip.

My hands learn to close.
I learn to pick up pieces
when dandelions scatter.

When I am small,
my father's hands are too quick to notice for long.

His constantly moving hands paint intricacies
onto tiny ships and tanks,
measure protein shakes, marinate steaks,
debone turkeys, scale fish, paint walls, roll dice.

His anxious hands grip firmly to the steering wheel
while I gaze out a rain drenched windowpane.
His hands safely deliver us to road trip destinations.

His purposeful hands fix something under the hood.
His focused hands meticulously count
tiny game pieces and slip them into bags
and seal them up, secure; double count just to be sure.

His proud hands solidly salute men at the gate.
I imagine him building bombs, steadily waiting to turn the key
with practiced hands, somewhere far away from me.

Sometimes hands are stones – so closed,
a shadow where no light escapes.
In every clutch, conviction.

How fortress fists
contort and twist
to keep things.

My hands learn to open.
I learn to pick at wall cracks
when rigid rocks erode.

When I am small,
I notice my parents' hands on sunny mornings.

Two sets of hands merge into one single-minded purpose;
to tickle me until breath becomes laughter,
and to hold me in from the wide world.

Small

A candy wrapper discarded on the floor,
forgotten breakfast dishes,
sooty shoe marks by the back door,
paper scraps trodden into carpet,
sticker residue on walls.

Thank you for the messes –
the signs of a child.
The little things left behind,
which will one day
be distantly behind us.

Wood

I miss ballet class —
the music mostly.
As the hard piano keeps tempo,
a dark down beat tells you to exhale
and bend and then
exult.

Each foot —
bound in lambswool
with pink satin skin
and ribbon-tied shins.

You don't need a coach
screaming commands,
veins pounding his neck.
The music compels you all on its own;
if you don't move, you are left behind,
cast aside,
asunder.

Each torso –
a vessel
as archaic language pours
from each branching limb.

Does your body imitate art,
or the other way round?
How a generational knowing
takes root in your core
as you dance.

Each toe box –
a stiff wooden joint
worn in delicate pain
for elegant pointe.

Dormant

Your malaise is rain
that permeates the path
and makes stepping forward futile.

Your heartbreak is thunder
that gathers friction
with no recourse but to strike.

Your anguish is lightning
that chokes the air
and leaves hollow scars.

I am a kite string in wind
that tangles in tree limbs,
stitching sorrow closed.

I am an empty grief
that sits in ear-ringing silence
after storms subside.

I am a seed in your clenched fist,
dry and hard as stone,
kept in dark to die.

Spring

Look for me beneath the ice.
Beneath ice, I'm held fast all winter.
All winter, my fast beating heart holds still.
Better to still my heart than hold a bleeding heart still beating.

Still, look beneath the ice once more.
Once more, a stirring pulse persists.
A pulse persists to stir the sun.
Sun stirs against pale ice until ice pales and melts.

When ice melts, might I emerge?
Emerge from melting ice that murmurs.
Murmurs of ice soon move to fissures.
Fissures will murmur – *time to move.*

Hidden

The art museum –
bookshelves brimming
with sensuous symbols;
humble humanity.

My shape reflected
in pottery;
clay curves,
fleshy figurines,
holy hedonists.

Feminine force
turned tiny,
miniaturized,
tucked away
from the architect's eyes.

Goddesses in small packages.

Stir

The deity of sleep I now entreat –
no rune-etched stones with messages to gain –
to stir from slumber deep as dreams retreat.

In shower's torrent with tile beneath my feet,
casting lots in loose hairs scribbling the drain,
the deity of sleep I now entreat.

No scrying mirror with wise insights to greet;
I gaze instead in mugs with gritty stains
to stir from slumber deep as dreams retreat.

Rather than candle flames and visions in the heat,
brewed coffee's steam dispels the drowsy brain.
The deity of sleep I now entreat.

In lieu of ancient altars and offerings of meat,
an athame cuts through squares of toasted grain
to stir from slumber deep as dreams retreat.

With rituals of shower, sip, and eat –
with divination tools of the mundane –
the deity of sleep I now entreat
to stir from slumber deep as dreams retreat.

Pare

Welcome to the Mind Salon –
choose from a thoughtful menu
of psyche soothing spa services.

Trim –
snip away
pesky synapses
that no longer serve you.

Color –
transform that gray matter into
semipermanent shades
and alter perceptions.

Updo –
fasten flyaway brain folds
into appealing shapes
and tamp down intrusive thoughts.

Facial –
cleanse,
exfoliate,
extract impurities, and
peel away painful memories.

Mask –
retain your favorite
unseemly beliefs
but hide them from prying eyes
behind an ethically sourced clay mask.

Wax –
remove
excess cilia
for a relaxing brain break.

Massage –
enjoy
gentle manipulation
of your ridges and grooves
and knead neural pathways to leave you like new.

New

Once – words ripped from sorrow,
driven deep into paper
like cutting flesh.
Red with pain and heat, bleeding,
fragmented and fleeting,
too sharp to stay.
Words beaten, broken, raw.

Now – words pure, thoughtful,
bloom like feathers plumed.
Wilting like dew-drenched grass,
then drying, gleaming anew,
winding through dark
tunnels toward light.
Words whole and safe and sound.

Morning

Stillness –
sky begins to lighten.
A yawning horizon
stretches into colors.

I fail to sleep this night,
suspended in twilight.
You speak of things I long to hear,
and before long,
the dawn
encroaches.

Your words like dreams
linger
in the silence,
and now I'm roused.
Renewed, I rise.

Bee

We can view
a million hues
when light waves reach
our eyes.
No wonder
we've adapted
to compartmentalize.

The rivalry –
it starts early
with pink or blue reveals,
teams in gym class
picked first or last,
grade-school halls of fame,
instilling pride or shame.

Superheroes – take your pick:
Batman tropes or Superman schtick?
Vicarious pride
when the bad guys died.
Mirrored in wars
on "other" shores,
or only in comic-book stores?

Wearing colors of our favorite team,
fuming at the TV screen
when our guy drops the ball.
Arbitrary loyalty;
the players aren't "ours" at all.

Fortnite squads, and AirPods,
our cars, our alma mater –
consumer choice – our fodder.
Superior brands,
self-righteous stans,
virtue signaling by name.
Pepsi or coke?
The best kept joke –
both profit just the same.

Bees can see a purple shade
hidden from human sight.
Bees choose direction based on
polarized patterns of light.
To limit light to just one side,
restricted to one plane;
the filters we put in place
make our perceptions change.

No wonder we're preoccupied,
constrained to red or blue.
An optic lens long overused –
the rivalry of me versus you.

We can't perceive
the purple of bees
and so it doesn't matter;
through limited hues
of win or lose,
we've yet to choose
an invisible "better."

I wonder –
will we cancel out,
or amplify,
when your and my (our)
light waves mix together?

23

GROW

Crescent

Moonlight changes
sometimes slender
often obtuse
morphing light and dark
wax and wane
suspended overhead
shifting shape and size
yet always held in place
never turning face
to see a different view.

Pocket

The pockets on dresses;
what trinkets within?
A marble, a matchstick,
a little girl spins.

The secretive sling bag;
what teenage desires?
A love note, a lip balm,
a girlfriend conspires.

The college kid's backpack;
what passion ignites?
A highlighter, Hawthorne,
a new poet writes.

The serious briefcase;
what grown-up demands?
A credit card, coffee,
two hard-working hands.

The mom bag encumbered;
with *why, mommy, why?*
From bottles to Barbies
in the blink of an eye.

The hand-me-down rucksack;
where will you roam?
A camera, a compass,
a daughter comes home.

My heart;
a container of faded knickknacks.
Now empty my pockets,
take me back, take me back.

Fire

Recipe for a Broken Heart:

1 cup hot sauce
wrongly labeled cherry juice.

2 ounces vodka
set on fire.

3 tablespoons dark chocolate
mixed with chunks of concrete.

4 marshmallows
doused in gasoline and burned beyond recognition.

5 ounces of raw steak
left out to bleed and eventually turn gray.

Garnish with pickled artichoke hearts –
heavy on the "choke."

Due

They say you shouldn't let anyone
live rent free in your head,
but what about me?
How do I make me pay
or go away?

I'm an overbearing landlord
lording over me.

Dwelling in the recesses
with shrouded eyes and windows,
my walls and shoulders cave.
My jaw and doors stay deadbolted.

My laugh is locked in the back room
and I won't give me the key.
I once used mirrors to see me;
now I only see a mere me I'm not used to.

My tears are a drippy faucet
in need of tightening
and I charge me extra
for each wasted drop.

River

Bare feet wander,
firmly forced upon the ground;
worn down,
heavier with every step.

With every step,
sink into rushing water.
Contemplate
weightlessness.

If I had a river
so long I'd never touch land again,
I'd lay down in the river.
I'd leave my bones behind.
I'd sink my face into the river
so tears would simply become water.

If I had a river
so long I'd never touch land again,
I'd slip along its sediment.
I'd let it shape me smooth like stones;
rough edges, sorrows planed away.

Imagine floating down the river –
rushing sounds fill your mouth.
Surrender voice.
Surrender choice.
No use fighting against the current;
course could change at any moment.

If I had a river
so long I'd never touch land again,
I'd trade my feet for driftwood.
I'd let the river choose.

Noon

Gold-rimmed clouds converge
and dissipate in turn.
Elongated shadows
shapeshift
as vapor-wisps
curl past.

I stand fastened –
a pillar
as air moves.

Shallow puddles bend light,
solid and liquid in turn.
Reflective ripples
mirror the sun
as it passes
overhead.

I am rooted to the earth,
a gnomon
as daylight climbs.

Morning wanes
and shadows gain.
Still, I remain.

Summer

An orb of hail descends
to nestle in green grass,
slowly seeping under sun,
weeping into wet and warm.

Brutal ice remade –
vibrant light begins one day
and roaring storm another.

Aestas tries on different outfits,
changing, shifting,
forcing us to take notice:
Rejoice.
Anticipate.
Listen.

Clay

Shape me as you like,
sculpt your heart's desire,
knead my every need,
and feed the passionate pyre.

Paint patterns on my skin,
etch your signature on my soul,
throw me into the kiln,
and fire me 'til I'm whole.

Meld me
to you.

Steady

I know I will find	I know I will find
him alone at the table,	her crashing through the kitchen
slurping cereal	at the break of dawn,
from a plain white bowl	immediately
while checking text messages;	wide awake and quick to task
it's always the same.	while I'm still drowsy.
Doesn't he ever tire	Would she like to sit
of his morning ritual?	still long enough to savor
Does he want some toast?	this untrodden hour?
I will find	I will find
his socks in the top drawer;	she's organizing again,
neat, folded, black stacks.	reinventing things.
Shirts in the closet;	New colors and styles –
moisture-wicking, polo tees,	where last week hung gothic chic,
twenty of the same.	now – peasant blouses.
Has he ever had the urge	Does this constant change
to wear socks with polka-dots?	bring her any closer to
Or a panda print?	loving her own skin?

I know I will find
him lying in bed at night
propped on his right side.
All night long he'll doze,
never bothered by a sound,
perfectly content.
Won't he ever try
a different position?
Sleep on his stomach?

I know I will find
her sitting at the bedside,
legs curled underneath,
worn down by her thoughts,
anxieties winning out
over connection.
Would it help if I
hugged her, or left her alone?
What choice is the best?

I still find
him waiting for me right there,
where he said he'd be;
so predictable,
honest, dependable, and
never a surprise.
Has he ever lied
or wanted to hide away
from expectations?

I still find
she's waiting for me at home,
dinner on the plate.
After a long day,
she's so thoughtful and sincere;
cooking just for me.
Does she know just how
eagerly I wait all day
to step through her door?

I love finding	I love finding
little things I never knew;	little things you think I don't
secret parts of you.	notice, but I do.
Doodles that you drew	How your smile reaches
in high school when the world	to the corners of your eyes,
was new and so were you.	bright when you laugh.
Can you get back there,	Do you know I smile
where uncertainty once lived?	when you hide behind my hand
Habits yet unset?	during scary scenes?
I know I will find	I know I will find
his peace infuriating	she's fiercely articulate
when I want a fight.	when she makes a point,
Petty arguments	but I seldom can
soften against reposeful,	understand why everything
unwavering walls.	is intense to her.
Does he ever feel	Can't she clearly see
emotions too strong to stay	how easily emotions
trapped in his body?	stain words with regret?

In him I find	In her I find
a safe place to be myself;	she loves me the way I am;
no prerequisite.	no prerequisite.
Steadfast love despite	Steadfast love despite
all the shifting moods I bring;	my bad jokes that make her scoff
ceaseless, he endures.	or outright insult.
Does he ever doubt –	Does she ever wish
what if I'm not good for him?	she could slow down her pace
How can he be sure?	and share jokes with me?
I know	I know
your calm arms will keep me still	I'm your calm after the storm;
when my mind's a whirl.	your stress slips away.
Always so certain	Perhaps if I stay
of your heart – your love for me	steadfastly your biggest fan,
never faltering.	you'll accept your worth.
Have you ever wished	Can you see it yet –
I could be steady like you?	how I've loved you all along?
Can you teach me now?	Let me show you how.

Lover

I wish that I could paint the sky the color of your eyes
and etch your radiant, loving smile into each sunrise.
I wish that I could sail your name far off into the sea;
all the waves and sand and spray would send it back to me.

I wish that I could hide your heart deep within the earth
and watch it blossom out in spring with every flower's birth.
I wish that I could make the mountains echo out your song;
and then I'd listen to your voice each day, and all night long.

I wish that I could store your kisses in every drop of rain,
and when the drops fall on my face, you'd kiss away my pain.
I wish that I could put your laughter high up in the trees;
they'd rustle with the happy sound fluttering on the breeze.

I wish that I could fill the starlight with your strong embrace;
at night, your tender hugs would bring warmth to all of space.
And if I could you'd be my world, you'd be in all I see –
and then that way, no matter what, you'd always be with me.

Go

Putting my history in a box –
an exercise in letting go
while holding on.

One box for souvenirs, brochures, timelining travels,
doodles, trinkets, '90s relics, childhood memories.

Another box for greetings from faraway friends and family,
folded up notes capturing adolescent whims,
glittery cards, scrapbooks, photographs without filters.

One more box for wedding artifacts, love letters, poems,
dreams fulfilled, promises kept.

A final box for outgrown baby baubles, scribbled scraps
of paper from my daughter saying *I love you*
in pictures and words.

Putting my history in a box.
Finding out my history is not only mine –
an exercise in letting go
to make more room for holding on.

Sail

When Wonders never cease
and ships neglect to moor,
we roam a vast abyss
and fail to recall shore.

Untethered tides aspire
to billow to Beyond,
casting off desires
we once considered fond.

For why would Wonders wish
for lands hitherto known,
when untold routes unfurl
and banish thoughts of home?

When Wonders overflow,
submerging well-worn paths,
familiar ways to go
are relics of the past.

So keep an even keel   45
though charts we now abandon;
let headwinds overtake the helm
toward depths we cannot fathom.

FLOWER

Autumn

Crisp air fashions frost
from stolen breath
as cascades of tiny gems
break underfoot.

Bare bone branches jut
from yellow orange skins
as hollow sunlight filters through the few
lingering leaves,
soon-to-be sloughed off.

Each time,
the world dies
beautifully.

Impe

When last you asked to meet,
I feigned a stomachache to stay inside –
remembering the way you turned my bruises
into lip balm cupped in your nimble palm.

The eerie means by which you mold
undesirable traits into gilded shapes.

Instead I follow you at dusk
as you creep, shifting
out of human skin
under receding sunlight.

A fire lit at forest's fringe
reveals your rumpled figure emerging out of shadows
as glowing ash capers with you, eager at secret's brink.

The skin you wear by day falls away
as moonlight slits your mask
illuminating a knobby leathered head,
trenchant ears, green-blue hue.

From firelight and pall of smoke extend
your stilt-like legs; protruding branches
which lope and jeer at flames,
nearly ablaze.

Sap-dappled dripping leaves appear
where once were fingers;
as you enact a feral jig, leaves flutter down
transformed to brown rot at your feet.

Golden tufts of straw like stubble
peek out from crumpled eyes and stilted smile,
while your true name
settles on my tongue.

Stilts
and rumpled skin.
Rumpelstiltskin.
So you're undone.

Womb

Hey only man,
will you be lonely, man?
When all your women die?
In protection of some sacred babes
they'll never rock-a-bye?

Hey only man,
let me tell you, man –
the only women I
have known to end a pregnancy
were ones who would have died.

The child who was raped
who would have died in childbirth,
her pelvic bones not wide enough
to summon a human's girth.

The already-a-mother
with an ectopic scare;
would you rather she left her breathing kids
for one that would never breathe air?

The late-term mother
who finds her wanted child
is still inside her and is dead.
And if she's forced to carry it,
she'd rather slit her wrists instead.

Hey only man,
do you know how lonely, man,
is a woman with a womb?
The hollow space
where in its place
is potentially her tomb.

Mother

Lanky lively legs.
A toss of titian hair.
Rain boots beat the floor.
Fast, fast, fast –
race out the back door.

Cheerful cadenced clink
of silver swing set chains.
My confident child.
Fly, fly, fly –
soar carefree and wild.

Wispy waning warmth.
Tall trees stretch shadow hands.
Day soon to be done.
Slow, slow, slow –
retreat with the sun.

A minute more to play.
Stay, stay, stay.

Promise

Sunlight peeking through curtains
Turning book pages
A kiss goodbye
Cold, clean water
A sleeping dog
Frost-crunched grass
One new egg
Ducks playing
A daughter's sleepy smile
Blueberries
Birds at the feeder
A text from a friend
Stretchy socks
Green leaves
A promise

Reach

Tuesday morning,
the library doors open
and the mothers of babies converge.

As I browse books,
the moms meander
while mini-humans
cling to shirt hems.

Hushed tones,
unhurried steps,
tinkling voices curious –
mama, lift me up so I can see!

Simple requests,
presently absorbed
with their mama.
The entire world is now.

Thin books in my palm –
no need to read a longer story.
I know how it ends;
small snippets at a time.

Her childhood is fading.
I think that, if she were to leave,
this is the beginning
of how it feels
to lose a child.

To walk a public place
with unsuspecting mothers,
to want to shake
and make them realize –
this moment slips away.

Until one day,
no matter what you do,
they will not cling to you.
No longer can you lift them up
even if they stay.

Metal

I can't quite put my finger on it,
but my heart is falling to pieces.

My daughter is growing too fast
and I'm fearful of the unknown.
On the one hand,
I want to trust and validate and believe in her;
but on the other hand,
I want to protect her from herself.
I know she will win in the end
and I'm grieving the loss.
No one could have prepared me for motherhood.
But I'm here now and it hurts.

I can't quite put my finger on it,
but I'm crying more than I should.

My body doesn't cooperate
with my brain the way it used to.
My brain says I'm clever and sexy and carefree,
but my body says I eat too many carbs
and my back hurts
and my pants don't fit.
I took an InTeRnEt QuiZ today,
which of course is TRUTH,
and it confirms:
I'm in fact a poison dart frog —
elusive, quick, and toxic.

I can't quite put my finger on it,
but sometimes I imagine the worst.

I will never write the book;
ChatGPT wrote a better one anyway.
I will never travel;
If you've seen one, you've seen them all.
I will never be fulfilled;
and my anger
will soon fade to sadness
will soon fade to apathy.

I can't quite put my finger on it,
but something propels me forward.

The sunrise mirrored on mountains.
The peace when I slip into bed.
I keep being curious
about tomorrow.
And someone brings me a smile,
or a lesson to learn.
And I open new eyes to forget –
set aside heartache, mistakes, regret –
in pursuit of what I can't quite
put my finger on.

Evening

An ode to observe belated blooms –
scatter of seeds past the farmer's moon,
drizzle of droplets from a feeble hose,
sunburnt leaves left too long exposed.

An ode to honor departed dreams –
expired rivers withered to streams,
hardened husks of last season's plot,
wrestling roots of crowded crops.

An ode to applaud sowing late –
scanty soil of uncertain fate,
behindhand buds coaxed from ground,
vying verdure though weeds abound.

An ode to extol slow success –
yawning flowers following rest,
meager harvest preceded by blight,
fruit that's sweetest when overripe.

Furrow

Little by little, I choose solid things.
My choices become rooted
in the rivers,
now canyons in my mind.
No ambiguity, no blurry edges left.
Only tight seams,
double knots just to be sure.
To feel secure; grounded.

One path, one trail ahead.
Inescapable, like a microscopic ant
crawling along the grooves of a walnut shell.
Yet the ant's feet can cling to walls,
walking sideways to escape the deep.
Whereas my feet
adhere to the same spot.
Tethered.

A collection of soft, safe edges
insulate the memories,
stifle the emotions,
soak up stray moisture.
What happens
when I pull a string?
When the edges fray?

I'm afraid
I will peek inside
the threadbare pouches
and I will not recognize
the white cloudy fluff,
now insubstantial.
But at least I kept them dry.

Gibbous

Driving to work this morning –
sun glows on my left.
Song comes on the radio,
reminding me of our early dating life
when intimacy meant staying up all night
asking questions, growing into knowing
each other's thoughts.

And last night I cried on your shoulder,
felt the tide of parenting –
a muddled, messy disaster.
I confided my insecurities, shame, fear;
you cheered me up with flirty banter, jokes,
made me feel safe and silly.

You encouraged me with the type of words
only my partner could give.
I realized parenting with my lover
through phase after phase
is its own kind of intimacy –
expanding, gaining over time.

The song, the radio, the new morning.
The second chance to try again
and be fuller than I was yesterday.
The knowledge that you see me
and you know I can do this,
even when I doubt it myself.

Bloom

And they lived happily ever after.

And they sent each other funny, borderline inappropriate
memes to make the workday and the time spent apart
slightly more bearable ever after.

And they fell asleep slumped together on the couch
in front of their favorite shows which they would have to
rewatch the next night ever after.

And they only occasionally cheated
and watched a couple episodes ahead
while the other was out of town ever after.

And they at least lived complacently ever after,
or satisfactorily ever after.

And they couldn't decide
what to eat for dinner ever after.

And they grudgingly cleaned up after each other
after complaining about it ever after.

And they perpetually washed dishes
with increasingly papery hands ever after.
And without ever discussing it aloud, they always slept
on their respective side of the bed every night ever after.

And they reflexively referred to themselves
as Us or We and never I nor Me ever after.

And they lived not too discontentedly
with their choices ever after.

And they never commented on the other's
fluctuating weight or burnt dinners
or unfortunate haircuts ever after.

And they spent long car rides conjecturing
about life and true crime and dream vacations
and which brand of laundry detergent was best ever after.

And they tried but often failed
to remember to say *I love you* ever after.

And they gathered up all the ever afters
and kept them safe and snug in a sack of happily.

And they tended to the ever afters twice a day,
and three times on Sunday.

And the ever afters grew about as much happily as is to be
expected from a well-cared-for collection of ever afters.

The End.

Chance

Thank you for connections, coffee, conversations,
and checking in and meaningful advice and meaning.

Thank you for safety, counselors, medication,
and blankets and warm clothes and warmth.

Thank you for snow, sunshine, amaryllis blooms,
and time alone and time to rest and rest.

Thank you for laughter, stories, braiding her hair,
and books and secondhand books and second chances.

FRUIT

Peel

I plotted out a patch of dirt
where once flowers unfurled;
I burned a box of red candles
to warm the wintry world.

And where I dug into the dirt
a single space for seed,
I melted drips of candle wax
to see if earth might bleed.

My weak attempt to contrive warmth
where only winter is known
as nature scoffs, unfolding
in its time – not my own.

So nothing grew from dirt
when plotting against the sun,
until wild spring returned
to reveal my plans undone.

How time alone might heal,
how seasons might discern,
how frail our semblance of control.
How lovely to unlearn.

Full

Recipe for Self-Acceptance:

Step One –
set these ingredients on the left side of your counter:
your parents' disappointment in you,
your ex-boyfriend's judgments,
society's standards,
and your own insecurities.

Step Two –
set these ingredients on the right side of your counter:
your genuine smile,
your heartfelt laughter,
that one time you felt confident and comfortable
in your own skin,
and your contagious charisma.

Step Three –
preheat the oven to soul-warming.

Step Four –
peel apart and detach your body weight from your self-worth
(reserve extra time for this step).

Step Five –
put all ingredients from the left side of the counter
into a large mixing bowl and beat vigorously.
Macerate the mixture with a dash of painful embarrassment
and a strong pinch of unfulfilled hopes.

Step Six –
dump the mixing bowl into the trash and set it on fire.
Help stoke the flame by dancing around
like a wild woman whooping at the top of your lungs.
Remember – fire needs oxygen.

Step Seven –
put all ingredients from the right side of the counter
into a baking dish and use your innate sense of self
to stir the ingredients until well mixed.
Set aside until dough rises into your accepted view of reality.

Step Eight –
once the oven is preheated,
place the baking dish on the center rack.

Step Nine –
set a timer for a future time
when you have learned to rely on your own intuition
and no one else's opinion of you matters.

Step Ten –
when timer dings, remove from oven.
Let cool and enjoy.

Reap

Atop your desk rests
a yellow squishy stress ball,
smiling and unstressed.

In your drawer waits
a stopped silver pocket watch,
contentedly late.

In your pocket sits
a snowy blank business card,
blithely titleless.

When their work did cease,
your busy relics resigned
to find time for peace.

Winter

Winter is for rest.
Ice crystals creep at each door.
Breath cannot escape unseen.
Sun sets beyond bare branches and
day ends before the final meal.
Life seeps away with each brittle break
and each receding hour of daylight.
Sheltering burrows of blankets,
things hidden away, awaiting gifts…

Winter is for stillness.
Sounds suspended in brisk air,
echoes of movement
against an abandoned landscape.
The earth beneath toughens
to ward away death.
None can grow here; all must grow within now.
Nothing stirs in Holda's house,
yet there is an unsettling…

Winter is for solitude.
The in-between moments.
The quiet spaces, contemplative.

Alone – forgotten youth of a past season;
winter's subtle lesson.
More than cold and dark,
warmth and light held within.
Draw down sun to hearth.
Warm darkness until it cracks open…

Winter is for now.
Quiet won't last forever.
Now is the moment to greet the way forward.
Pause long enough to notice –
breathe in understanding; breathe out.
Learn to be still and see beyond
the supposed emptiness.
You must make yourself empty
to receive what comes…

Winter is for recalling spring.

Crone

Waking to new snowfall,
to the realization
plans are paused today.

Ambitious travels cease,
inclined instead to stay
in my duvet.

Assuredly I would have gone
on an adventure
if not for the
soft white descent
of eiderdown
upon the ground.

So I decline to venture
past the windowpanes.

Carry

Black boots —
hard rubber grips underfoot,
laced up tight,
snug against wool socks,
waterproof.
Rock and forest and city proof.
Well suited to travel
a bucket list trip
beyond history and time,
to make an imprint
that lasts.
Durable, real, hard, lingering.
Peat fire scent
and green tinge of moss
left behind in the soles.

Night

Four books on my nightstand
make four corners
connected to four memories
of strong women far away in the world
but also beside me in the
four books on my nightstand.

A gift from my sister; plot perplexing,
woven with ancient myth
to which modern times still cling.

A gift from a female acquaintance;
a wish list, a surprise, a smile, a simple black cover,
an author's life carved out of poetry.

A borrowed gift inspired by
a woman's photograph, curiosity.
Unbeknownst to her – just what I was looking for.

A book-club-gifted-book
about an old man and sadness
read by a group of women, all sharing a singular experience.

Four books on my nightstand
stand for our connection,
stand for my immense gratitude for this connection,
stand for solidarity – expanding and expansive.

I am inspired by the same thoughts
that inspire others.
I know a secret to life –
to always seek out the thing to be grateful for.

Four books on my nightstand
stand together even on the darkest nights
when the dark of the world seems unbearable.
The four books on my nightstand stand for light.

Husk

Moving out of a house
is like observing the dead body of a loved one.

You recall there once was something alive there,
something there to love,
but now it's an empty husk.

A desolate wave crashes over you
as you realize the unsettling way the house feels.
Not the comfort you once longed for,
not the familiar tug drawing you in,
not the warm glowing semblance of a life.

So how can you miss the physical shell that you've outgrown?

Detached
memories disconnected from
the place.

What you hold in your hand
and what lies beneath your feet
pale in comparison
to the past impression left behind in your mind.

It's not yours anymore.
Time to go.

Time

Through a gold-rimmed awning, an arrow
of sunlight cascades through the window
where buzzing green blossoms and garden rows
fill the glass pane.
Wooden frames overflow in abundance with no
end to warm summer rays.

The moon's stolid face seeks to raise
you from sleep. Compelled, you climb a narrow
casement ledge and peer over the edge with no
latch to hold back the gaping window
thrown wide – a precarious pane
of stained glass, red as a rose.

A dark expanse awaits; endless rows
of kaleidoscope stars and cryptic cosmic arrays
encased in a dormer pane.
A comet streaks like an arrow
past your thin window,
too fast to stay and too vast to know.

A wind-battered porthole is no
barricade against cruel swells that rose
from the depths to rattle the window
held fast. Nature's wrath will raze
to the ground your flimsy round mirror. A narrow
sheet of glass is all that separates you from pain.

Ghosts of handprints remain on the pane
as spirals of ice make the panel opaque – no
longer concealing the cold. Crystals cling to a narrow
seam, forbidding your touch like a rose
thorn that threatens – until thawing rays
cause fleeting frost to withdraw from the window.

At last – an old, moldering window;
a skylight with spiderweb cracks in the pane.
Peeling paint curls away from the frame as you raise
rusty hinges with trembling weight. You no
longer wait for your fate. In escape, you rose
to the sill and flew true as an arrow.

Each window, a witness – to know
your familiar face in the pane, reflected in infinite rows
until time's enlightening rays grow ever more narrow.

Lost

Age 0

My baby teeth
My early memories
My childhood friends
My playing pretend
My music box
My collection of rocks
My favorite gloves
My dog I loved

Age 10

My innocence
My confidence
My awkward shame
My dreams of fame
My class ring
My *I know everything*
My good eyesight
My need to always be right
My appetite

Age 20   My hunger cues
My dance moves
My small waistline
My spare time
My religion
My indecision
My being "fake"
My desire to stay up late
My ability to roller-skate
My sewing kit
My cool
My shit

Age 30   My fear
My distrust
My perky bust
My constant worry
My "in a hurry"
My fragility
My insecurity
My need to people-please

Today   My car keys

Expanse

I love how blue can drown you –
hold you under with indifferent force
to make lips match its hue.
Ice on a desolate beryl sea.
Underneath – a deeper shade,
all the way to black.

I love how blue can stretch out, endless –
blinding sapphire brilliance,
wind on a cloudless expanse,
a sparse sky bleeding into white
with the sun until it's gone.
Dispersing into galaxies.

I love how blue can feed the green –
azure above, within, below.
Nourishing the spindly fern,
craggy pine, fuzzy moss,
the lush soaked canopy.
Foliage devouring so much air.

I love how blue deceives you.
When astronauts peer at the earth
from far away – the innocuous, beguiling orb
where shades of cobalt swirl and blend
into a mass of life and death
bound in an amniotic sac
of atmosphere and gravity,
tethered to space and time
within a limitless beyond.

Do other stars hold turquoise in their satellites?
The small cerulean marble held with a string
like cats batting strands of yarn
leaving the mass to arc across the floor,
ever near?

I love imagining how blue will end.
When the sun absorbs us,
there will be a moment
when it too loves blue.

Water

Emotions are the water
and I learn to be the levee.
The cost of letting in the good
is the bad seeps in as well.
A soft drizzle, or torrential rains?
Hard to tell.

Each experience –
a trickle of water in the mind.
First only a stream, but in time,
streams carve rivers,
etch trails, erode deeper paths.
Until the choices you make
are set before you.

One day, a boy asks me to a dance.
He holds me so gently;
I'm a hazy cloud
in danger of dissipating.
I distill his smile
into a cotton, heart-shaped pouch
with white yarn
and a drawstring at the top,
drawing this moment down
safe and sound, tucked away.

The last time in my grandma's house,
I hold her coffee cup in my hands like the cloud.
Like trying to hold a water droplet
before it absorbs into the skin.
I take a needle and thread
and stitch up my grandmother's picture frames,
her set of dominoes, her scarves and earrings,
and the magnolia trees in the backyard.
I sew them into a tiny satin pillowcase,
full of cotton batting.
Will tears ruin the satin?
To be safe, just in case,
I set it aside.

The whimsy of childhood
evaporates so quickly;
a sprinkler spraying
on the summer sidewalk.
I capture my drawings of fairies,
the cello, the ballet slippers,
and the carefree closeness with a girl
I might have liked to kiss.
I bundle them up in lambswool,
and weave it tightly into twine
to make a colorful welcome mat
to place my feet on
in my new house,
in my grown-up life.

EPILOGUE

A woman's lore:
Each poem a door –
arrive a maiden,
depart a crone.

She gathers words
o'er waxing moons.
Before – spring's birth.
Now – winter's hearth.

And flowers bright,
hold morning's light.
Noon, evening, night –
do guide her home.

ACKNOWLEDGMENTS

This collection would have remained a dormant seed if not for the thoughtful tending provided by a few key people.

To my editors – Beth and Vince – thank you for your professional insights and personal validation. You gave me the confidence to keep going.

To my early readers – Crystal, Gabby, Kate, Nat, and Tia – thank you for your attentive feedback when these pages were most vulnerable. You are among the visionary women who shape my world and inspire me to write.

To my family – Dave, Edd, Lori, and Quin – thank you for teaching me the important lessons, seeing and accepting me, and giving me a life worth celebrating.

And lastly – thank you to the readers, the dreamers, and the whimsy seekers. I hope you find a glimpse of yourself in Poesy Pate.

INDEX OF FIRST LINES

A candy wrapper discarded on the floor, ... 9
A poesy pate: 1
A woman's lore: 97
Age 0 My baby teeth 88
An ode to observe belated blooms – 61
An orb of hail descends 36
And they lived happily ever after. 66
Atop your desk rests 77
Bare feet wander, ... 32
Black boots – 81
Crisp air fashions frost 49
Did the princess ever have second thoughts? 5
Driving to work this morning – 64
Emotions are the water 92
Four books on my nightstand 82
Gold-rimmed clouds converge 34
Hey only man, ... 52
I can't quite put my finger on it, ... 58
I know I will find 38
I love how blue can drown you – 90
I miss ballet class – 10
I plotted out a patch of dirt 73
I wish that I could paint the sky the color of your eyes 42
Lanky lively legs. 54
Little by little, I choose solid things. 62

Look for me beneath the ice. 13
Moonlight changes 27
Moving out of a house 84
Once – words ripped from sorrow, ... 18
Putting my history in a box – 43
Recipe for a Broken Heart: 30
Recipe for Self-Acceptance: 74
Shape me as you like, ... 37
Stillness – 19
Sunlight peeking through curtains 55
Thank you for connections, coffee, conversations, ... 69
The art museum – 14
The deity of sleep I now entreat – 15
The pockets on dresses; 28
They say you shouldn't let anyone 31
Through a gold-rimmed awning, an arrow 86
Tuesday morning, ... 56
Waking to new snowfall, ... 80
We can view 20
Welcome to the Mind Salon – 16
When I am small, ... 6
When last you asked to meet, ... 50
When Wonders never cease 44
Winter is for rest. 78
Your malaise is rain 12

ABOUT THE AUTHOR

Natasha North lives in Colorado with her husband and daughter — along with their beloved pets, house plants, and board game collection. Natasha developed a fondness for traveling after living in two countries and eight states during her childhood. She has worked in education and local government as a teacher, curriculum specialist, and project manager. Her interests include gardening, games, and journaling. She previously published the short story "Love, a Tree," which explores themes of self-awareness and interconnectedness.